THE VINE TEMPLE

Books by Kathleen Driskell

Laughing Sickness

High Horse: Contemporary Writing by the MFA Faculty of Spalding University
    (co-editor with Sena Jeter Naslund)

Seed Across Snow: A Collection of Poems

Peck and Pock: A Graphic Poem
    (Illustrated by AJ Reinhart)

Next Door to the Dead: Poems

Blue Etiquette: Poems

Creativity & Compassion: Spalding Writers Celebrate 20 Years
    (co-editor with Katy Yocom)

Books in the Cox Family Poetry Chapbook Series

2021
Elegiac, Charles Seluzicki

2022
What Passes Here for Mountains, Matt Morton
This Long Winter, Joyce Sutphen

2023
The Vine Temple, Kathleen Driskell

THE VINE TEMPLE

Kathleen Driskell

The Cox Family Poetry Chapbook Series

Carnegie Mellon University Press
Pittsburgh 2023

ACKNOWLEDGMENTS

The Vine Temple by Kathleen Driskell is the fourth volume in The Cox Family Poetry Chapbook Series of Carnegie Mellon University Press. The Press administrators and staff express their profound appreciation to Courtney, Lisa, and Jordan Cox for their generous support.

The author would like to acknowledge and thank the editors of the following magazines for first publishing these poems:

Appalachian Review: "Blue Collar to Middle Class," "Tiara," "Jewish Cemetery, Prague," "River Walk in Winter" and "Psalm for the Heretic"
The New Yorker: "Poem for Grown Children"
Red Tree Review: "Pastoral" and "Praise for a Rabbi Who Lived Long Ago"
Symposeum Magazine: "Synonyms" and "Resurrection"

I'm also grateful to The Hermitage Artist Retreat which allowed me time and shelter to write many of these poems. Special thanks to my colleagues on the faculty of Spalding University's Naslund-Mann Graduate School of Writing who are always an inspiration to me. I would also like to express thanks to Connie Amoroso who has been marvelous to work with. I am foremost indebted to Jerry Costanzo, editor of Carnegie Mellon University Press for his interest and appreciation of my work. Without him, *The Vine Temple* wouldn't exist, would never have existed.

Book design by Connie Amoroso

Library of Congress Cataloging-in-Publication Data
Names: Driskell, Kathleen Mason, author.
Title: The vine temple / Kathleen Driskell.
Description: First. | Pittsburgh : Carnegie Mellon University Press, 2023. | Series: The Cox family poetry chapbook series | Summary: "*In The Vine Temple*, Kathleen Driskell invites readers to walk with her through past landscapes, including retreats to a Confederate cemetery near her turbulent childhood home and more recent hikes in a nearby park where the sacred and sublime reveals itself in the natural world. Driskell's poems examine the transmutability of human language and its ability to liberate, exhilarate, but also encourage some into terrible darkness"—Provided by publisher.
Identifiers: LCCN 2022043258 | ISBN 9780887486876 (trade paperback)
Subjects: LCGFT: Poetry.
Classification: LCC PS3604.R56583 V56 2023 | DDC 811/.6--dc23/eng/20220912
LC record available at https://lccn.loc.gov/2022043258

CONTENTS

REMEMBERING THE LOUISVILLE BUSSING RIOTS

At one side of Dixie Highway, standing
in the grass, white women, mothers and
daughters and sisters, their faces twisted,
expectorating saliva caught in newspaper

photographs like the crystal drops
of chandeliers. My memory is full
of sound as well, returning hisses, sticks
on a snare drum, or a radio that's lost its channel.

But the sound, too, of bus wheels rolling
over crushed glass, as the students advanced
slowly into dangerous foreign territory,
the parking lot of what had always been,
until then, a high school for whites only.

CONFEDERATE CEMETERY

I learned from the historic plaque
that the veterans buried in the small
section had not died as young men
in battle, but had succumbed nearby
in the Old Confederates Home
with gingerbread trim around its wide porch.
There, as kids like me pedaled past
on our way to the store to buy Bazooka,
death had come a calling.

Something I'd read must have helped me
realize the bones under my feet were
on the wrong side of it all, how else
would I have known, along with the slurs
at the dinner table, my neighborhood,
sprung up recently as a white asylum
from school desegregation, that things
were not as they said they were?

Still, in a house filled with shouting
and threats and heaved plates (the offending
meatloaf sliding down the wall, leaving
a wet smear as if a traitor had just been
executed in our kitchen), I solaced in
the tidiness, the unyielding order of those
markers, government issued, and aligned
painstakingly within that half acre.

HOMONYMS

In school. First grade perhaps? Maybe,
second. We are studying language.
Homonyms—now they are called homophones,
I think. Each child is asked to make a poster
to illustrate a pair of words that sound
the same but mean different things.

On one side of my poster board, I draw
a red-and-white striped ball. On the other,
the face of a child, pale, pink, eyes
squinted, tears spurting out across
the poster. Curly hair, like mine.

I shiver. What have I drawn? How
is it possible for one sound to do that,
to have one meaning that rises while
the other falls, like a schoolyard seesaw.
And this, though I knew it not
then, this metaphor for the life to come,
a seemingly bland perfect sphere, a toy,
potential for joy, watered by woe.

MILITARY HEADSTONES

On military headstones,
at the top, often a Christian cross
is incised into the gray granite,
and if you squint your eyes you see
cross, cross, cross, cross, cross, all
calling, *come on across*, and so on.

CONFEDERATE CROSS

Gone missing from Pewee Valley's
Confederate Cemetery were the young men
from our county killed in action, bodies
abandoned on the blood field, or those
who died from the bubbling green infections
ravaging camp hospitals far from
their Kentucky homes. Most young as the kids

being bussed from the inner city, all eyes
caught in the frames of bus windows
on a young white man, standing in the middle
of Louisville's Dixie Highway. (Dixie Die-way
we called it because of the countless crash
fatalities that had happened there.) He was
slick haired, parted hair curling around his ears,

cigarette hanging on lip. They watched him as
he lunged, again and again, thrusting
a flagpole with a Confederate cross sagging
from it, as if he were running into battle,
as if he wanted nothing more than to impale
each of the kids on the bus upon his bloody

shish kebab. As a kid, when I saw a car with
a Confederate flag bumper sticker, my first
thought, I admit, was redneck, not bigot.

BLUE COLLAR TO MIDDLE CLASS

My parents aspired to climb into the middle
class and cling tight. PTA, golf scrambles,
bridge. A frothy whiskey sour, plastic pink
spear, complete with hilt, driven through
the bright maraschino cherry and an orange
slice dropped atop and floating in chipped
ice, ordered whenever out with couples
who had learned to ask for their steaks
medium rare, sneering at the sweet French
dressing the waitress rattled off with options
for tossed salads. Instead, they requested
creamy Italian, just then in vogue.

The wives pulled the cherry stems through
their teeth and shook their heads. No,
of course, they won't allow their children
to be bussed—though, they did not think
of themselves as bigots. Hadn't they just come
of age in the Age of Aquarius? Hadn't they
rolled up the carpets in their living rooms,
pushed them against the walls, and allowed
Chubby Checker to teach them how to twist?

BURNT ORANGE

I don't think he actually hit her.
I learned, though, it doesn't matter
if the threat is always there. Hadn't he
reared back, hammer overhead, blue
eyes wild as Jesus's in the temple,
threatening to bash my brains in
when he'd called me down to
the basement to help him with the chore.

My crime? Standing there while he
was unable to loosen the rusted hose
from the washing machine. *Burnt orange,*
I remember thinking. I remember thinking
I will be killed in the basement of this house
where I have lived for twelve years,
with these people, but I will not flinch. And
then, of course, I did. Flinch. I mean.

PATTERN

I moved through the orderly rows of veteran
dead and thought about how each thin gray
headstone, high as my knees, was uniform
as the boots issued to all soldiers. I moved from
marker to marker, read the inscribed details,
names and death dates, those scratchings
that were unique but also so shallow it made it
no easier to conjure up the life, nor the flesh
that had been on the bones beneath my feet.

TIARA

As the Homecoming King escorted Brenda
across our football field, all heads, in unison,
turned from looking at her to Mr. Rausch,
our biology teacher, who sat with his wife
in the bleachers, his two little kids merrily
throwing popcorn at each other, laughing
and swinging their feet wildly.

Mrs. Rausch was so dour looking, so rumpled,
her hairdo a frizzy salon-frosted wedge,
that I'm sure most thought *well no wonder*
as we compared her to the beaming Miss
Oldham County Homecoming 1976. There
were insects whining in the halo of
the field's floodlights, but Brenda, her tiara,
her blue sateen gown with its princess
neckline, twinkled sweetly down below.

STATUARY

If both front feet of a horse
are reared in a statue, the rider
is presumed killed in battle.

If one front hoof is raised, the rider
is presumed wounded in battle.

If all four horse hooves stand firmly
on the ground, the rider died a natural death,
say in his sleep at the Old Confederates Home,
across the fence and down the road.

If a soldier limping toward home,
ends up dying alone in the brush,
there is no horse, no statue.

SYNONYMS

Though used interchangeably, as with most
synonyms there is a denotative
as well as a connotative difference
between a *graveyard* and a *cemetery*.

A graveyard rests beside a church: one
wanders from the pews and pulpit to visit
the still members of his congregation.

But one usually enters a cemetery
under a vine-covered arch, or sometimes
between pillars of brick and mortar
with carriage lights atop each.

There are gardens and religious
monuments, statues of saints, perhaps
a loose philosopher behind an old cedar,
and reflecting pools and winding paths
to be walked while introspecting.

Headstones mark the graves
of those laid to rest next to another with
whom they've likely never had a conversation,
much less an argument about Jesus,
and never will henceforth. Heaven.

RESURRECTION

And perhaps someday my own ashes
will be scattered through the meadows
of tickseed, carrot weed, and drooping dog
hobble, Kentucky wildflowers that I love.

A speck of me might be caught in the wind
and dropped like a flea into the cupped hand
of a bellflower, falling upon a beetle that has slipped
away and has fallen asleep within that blossom.

When later the beetle is eaten by the finch,
I might be swooped through the blue air of summer,
riding as high as any of the orthodox resurrected.

PARADOX

Ancient churches always seem
to be sinking, but any good docent
will tell you they aren't, rather the graveyards
next to them are rising as insects and time
churn busily, toiling to turn all to soil.

If one is buried in an ancient graveyard,
paradoxically, only then is it possible
to be lowered and lifted at the same time.

JEWISH CEMETERY, PRAGUE

I learned when I visited
the Jewish cemetery in Prague,
that the dead were relegated
to one plot behind their synagogue,
so small that layering graves became
the only way to give way for the new

dead; consequently, in that graveyard
the ground provides no mossy idyll.
All appears to be erupting, the headstones,
wrecked teeth, as if dead are struggling
to escape their coffins, as if the dead
have learned that for some
there is no place to be forgotten.

THE CARETAKER

Now when the grass needs cutting, the caretaker
comes with his new wife. I knew his old wife, who,
three years after their son's sudden death, was buried

next to her darling boy. Heart problems, I believe.
The new wife's hair, long and black, flips behind her.
Sitting in the saddle of the lawn mower, she steers

expertly, weaving around gravestones, as if practicing
dressage. He's following where she's just mown, swaying
as if he hears some melancholy music in his head while

he weedwacks around the plinths of his
wife and son. He reminds me of Frost's poem "Mowing,"
but instead of swinging a scythe, this mower's

life is measured by the whir of a weed
wacker. I'm stuffing pillowcases and bedsheets
into the washer and watching the couple

through the laundry room window. I'm measuring
out soap as I find myself wondering if when he
proposed to her he disclosed mowing this graveyard

every week from late March to early November
was part of the deal? Did he tell her that even
with a new wife there's no such thing as a new life?

LUCK

Your father and I said nothing
as we drove an hour to the hospital:

what could be said but small prayers
to gods we do not believe in. And

if we did mumble prayers, what images
of comfort could they offer? I saw red

fire trucks flashing. I saw when they arrived,
the firefighters had no need to pull

their ladders from their trucks. There was nowhere
to climb, no one to find at an open window.

Yesterday, I remember thinking we were so lucky.
I remember thinking that felt like a curse.

RIVER WALK IN WINTER

for Claudia Emerson

All is quiet here this morning.
It's too cold and early for runners,
though their kids are already
in yellow buses on the roads over there
beyond these woods.

No one is walking a dog,
yet, despite the wind, most
dogs would be here happily.

In the year or so before she died,
when able, she'd walk in a park
along a path next to a river,
somewhat like this,
and try not to think about cells
dividing. And growing. So odd
to think of growing as a negative.
Especially now. In winter, I mean.

She was loved again.

And, she loved him.

She loved dogs, too, but she grew
so angry, she said (she needn't have,
I heard the rage in her voice),
when they came bounding toward
her off their leashes, their owners
walking casually behind,
expecting everyone to be
as delighted as they
that they owned
such marvelous creatures.

I feel compelled to defend her,
to say again that she loved dogs.

To make sure that you heard me.

She loved all animals, really.

(She loved the whole fucking world.)

So maybe it was as those dogs
bounded toward her, they made her realize
just how easily, then, she could be completely
knocked off her feet
by what she loved.

TEMPLE

You see your own eye in the center
of the crow poison's blossom.

On the surface of the quiet pond,
articulated bugs create

circles of thought. There in the woods,
grapevines twist into a temple.

The darkness has grown you a door.
Walk through:

MOTH

I lay on the flowered davenport, my head in her lap,
to hear talk of the first husband who came home early
to find her suitcases and hatboxes ready at the door.

How he beat her until she lay curled like a sick old cat
on the linoleum floor of their kitchen, watching him drop
every hat she owned into a garbage can he'd set on fire.

Oh, how I loved stories like these. Like a brown moth, that
had tired of fluttering through the night, I landed, pressed
my wings against the warming glass of that kitchen door.

MORNING DEW

When the morning sun spills over the tip of
the hill, the autumn meadow which had
seemed so quiet, begins to flicker with light,
acres of wrecked webs suddenly visible,

all filaments now glistening with dewed
orbs. For as far as one can see,
one village after another, sacked by
marauders, who finding nothing more
to pillage have moved on.

Here and there, a mummified fly twirls in remain,
autumn stalks, sad filaments, sad strands unloosed
and trying to break free, slight fog rising as if
from smoldering ruined ashes— and then, one
web nearly perfect, facets intact, appears like
the glorious rose window of Notre Dame.

WHAT THE DEAD . . .

The dead must be more emphatic,
more clear-voiced while alive and willing to state
all manner of things. My grandmother
did not want to be cremated, that much
I knew, yet she came home with me in a small box.

If she'd revealed a place on earth she loved so well
as Jesus's heaven, I might have known where
to lower her casket. I might not have flinched
at the undertaker's questions. As it is, she sits on a shelf
with my children's mittens and worn ice skates.
As it is, she remains set among all kinds of temporal sin.

PASTORAL

On a warm day in winter, I walked
away from my unhappy flock
to skip through dried weed and

wave a wand, a stem of thorny black
locust, and then I stooped to watch a hare,
heart-beating through dusky fur

and then I dipped at the brown edge
of the pond where the heron raised
its spear, victoriously piked

with a wriggling fish.
I had been gone for days
when I saw God reach through

low cloud cover, his fingers skittering
in the brush, fingers like spider legs
running this way, then that.

I watched God's fingers stop
nonchalantly to rub out something
between thumb and pinky.

He may be able to drag me
back into the fold,
but I'm not going easily.

I'm waiting, ducked under
the sumac with the ruby-beaded tips.
I'm wearing a new coat

of wooly cockles and wielding
a torch ablaze with honey
and furious bees.

PSALM FOR THE HERETIC

The lord is my shepherd and leads me
to slaughter. Let's not pretend
otherwise. After all, my mind
is frilled with tomorrows.
Why ask me to love the lamb
seized for your Sunday supper?
Oh, God, grant me a calendar
blank as a sheep's.

PRAISE FOR A RABBI WHO LIVED LONG AGO

The Roman soldiers built a pyre
of dried wood, I imagine cypress,
then dragged the old Rabbi out.

He'd been wrapped like a mummy
in a Torah scroll. Two soldiers lashed him
to the stake, then touched a blazing torch

to the wood at his feet. "What do you see?"
his followers shouted as they stood among
a mob come to watch the old man burn.

Smoke rose and flames began to climb up
though the lines of scripture. He called back:
"The parchment is burning, but the words

are flying away." Thousands of miles
from that stone piazza, more than a thousand
years later, in the tradition of another religion,

but without faith in anything much, I sit on a beach, I
look out to nothing but continuing water, palms
out, waiting to catch bits of ash.

POEM FOR GROWN CHILDREN

In a poem I love, the husband slices open
a pepper to find a church,

but here at the sink I've found a house, and
inside, the rattling seeds of a chandelier.

It doesn't matter. My husband is too by himself
in the hospital, and in our home at the window I stand

alone for the first time in almost thirty years. Then,
he'd rushed out into the dark, summoned to

his father's deathbed. But I wasn't really alone.
My toddler son slept, his mouth slightly open

and red and wet inside like a fledgling's,
my daughter grew within me, close

as a locket on a chain. When my husband returned,
I remember he talked of the rattle. The death rattle.

The children are now inside their own homes
asleep, curled around their beloveds. But all so young

yet, they do not think we will ever die.
In their garden beds, if they are dreaming of seeds

and light, they are dreaming of little blazes
growing hotter. They are not dreaming of wind

and flickering. And, certainly, they are not
dreaming of smoke.